Growing up the most (relucta
town, Malaika Kegode cut h
opening for bands in music
LeftBank, sometimes in tre
audience's attention with her begu......ᵧ

Since those beginnings she has gone on to work closely with
organisations such as Apples and Snakes, Roundhouse and
BBC 1Xtra and is a member of the Raleigh Road Collective,
formed as part of 1Xtra's Words First initiative.

Malaika has performed around the country at theatres, music
venues, literary events and festivals such as WOMAD and
Boomtown. She inspires young people as a workshop facilitator.

Currently living in Bristol, where she feels happily less 'exotic',
she is creator and host of Milk Poetry, a regular thriving event
in the city.

Requite

Malaika Kegode

Illustrated by
Andreea Diana Stan

Burning Eye

Burning Eye Books
Never Knowingly
Mainstream

This edition published by Burning Eye Books 2016

www.burningeye.co.uk
@burningeyebooks

Burning Eye Books
15 West Hill, Portishead, BS20 6LG

ISBN 978-1-911570-04-2

For Liam

CONTENTS

STOWAWAY

a story

He worked in a petrol station, so he saw rainbows daily.
Not easily impressed was he by changing of seasons or
beauty in the weather, but she was called Summer, and she ignited
him.

She was a hippy girl, one of those free spirits who
rarely shave their legs, get existential about crystals and the moon.
Before she danced into his life in navy blue and long, dark feathers
he had forgotten how soft lips could be. Even more so when
pressed up against his skinny, pale body. She showed him a whole
new world on her ganja-scented settee, and he was stung.

But girls like this,
they can be dangerous. They fall for boys
because they can play the guitar and might seem
spontaneous, so she kissed anyone that she could.
Of course he thought that he was the only one
that she should because, okay, he might be some poor kid
from the grotty, dead-end part of town, but surely in her beautiful
mind she knew he was a good man, that he was kind.

She invited him to this party;
he knew all of her friends would be painfully, purposefully arty
but he went anyway, with a bottle of wine he bought for £5.99.

He got there and pushed through throngs of dyed hair, smoke,
acid tongues. Images began to form, the bodies in the hallways
all too forlorn and the girls all looked like her: same ripped tights,
knee-length skirts with whispered tales of mischief, just to make the
men stiff, and crowned Summer the masterful mistress of this,
with her famous poison kiss.

And she was there. Wearing some stranger's face, her eyes glowing
wide, an empty space. He saw for the first time her greed, how
every pore of her just wept with need

and realised she didn't need saving,
her lips were all that he was craving and
to flatter himself with chivalry seemed shameful.
So he fell onto the street, six beers down, still somehow
found his feet. For the first time, maybe ever, he felt
properly alone, looked up at the sky as it began to snow.

You can never really own a person, or stop a spirit from ascending.
You can't quell a bright spark in the hope it'll bring you a happy
ending but nature rewards you for solitude; if you can be your own
sun and moon then beauty, love, they will come to you soon.

And some people will stow away in your heart;
just remember that love doesn't have to be some high,
fine art.

All you really need is someone who can help you breathe.
All you really need is someone who's going to help you breathe.

TK

We used to trace lines of constellations with our fingertips,
make sense of logic with backwards nonsense,
mourn Sunday evenings on the school day ahead.

Not much has changed, only we drink
a little more gin now, a little less juice,
a little less cow's milk, a little more oat.
The smell of Superdrug cologne, its garish green box
has faded from my memory, now you only smell of
cigarettes and Hugo Boss.

You smell like our dad
and have his thumbs.
I don't think you use them to lick-flick stars anymore
or play *Tony Hawk's Pro Skater* after dark
with the sound turned down.

You adjusted your spine quicker than I did.
It cracked just as much, life filling the notches.
Still remember the day all six foot two of you fell
down to sleep. Made the floorboards rattle, beams cringe,
a personal Pompeii.

So I knew growing was hard,
a head pulled each way shrouded in cigarette smoke,
twenty-four Royals in your pocket but no crown.
When I watch you now, you drink slow
as though the bubbles that surge upwards in their headiness
carry uncertainty, as though the clawing on your tongue
is a reminder of pre-teen pints in country pubs
full of sweat.

So you drink slow,
I still wear black tights in the sun
to hide the things I have done.
Growing up was hard. But we always had the stars.

We both live in cities now, it's harder to see them.
So sometimes I trace the pinprick light
of the cityscape at night,
make a constellation,
and hope that you do the same.

BUBBLES

When the sky begins to change shape
and you learn to stop breathing under water,
perhaps the circumference of thigh you measured
with (limp) pieces of string will seem suddenly irrelevant,
your wrists will stop cracking their stoic melody
and life might seem worth moving for.

Perhaps this will happen.
You will stop walking backwards.

But for now I'm afraid sometimes
it is impossible for life not to seem
retrograded.
Learn to expect the way split lips feel like
rain on a hot day except
everything is under water.
Bubbles.
Fingertip ripples.

Once I watched a documentary about flying fish,
envied their patterns of gliding,
a lesson on how to fit in anywhere…
Stopped trying to fly,
I'm still teaching myself to stop breathing under water.

Being all green and blue and hungry and lonely,
discipline can teach you to wave whilst drowning,
not to swallow the tide or feel reeds between your teeth.
I have always loved the sea.
I believe I always will, even if it envelops me.

MUSIC

Another cup of tea is poured;
we sit, watch the steam form coils
in the silent space between us.

I get this from my mother, who in turn
from her father learnt the South London
stoicism of awkward vulnerability and
maybe you need more than a bacon sandwich,
this fifth cup of tea, but my arms fail to reach out,
lips cannot find comforting words, I cannot be the alcove
of warmth your sadness deserves.
Affectionate love can make my head spin
and tangle… But I can put on YouTube and watch red buffer
hope.

Because I believe in Kanye West the way some do in Keats,
believe in Marshall Mathers the way some do in Milton –
I was born into a world where Slick Rick was king
and taught that music is the best medicine for
pretty much anything.

So to show my adoration, my affection,
listen to this song because it reminded me of you.
Listen to this song, because it reminded me of you.
And surely that is the greatest acclaim,
that every note, beat and rhyme makes me think
of your face, think of your name.

I don't remember my parents loving each other
but I remember them loving music,
the comfort the melody brings,
socks sliding on the cold floors of warm kitchens
in imitation moonwalks we called sun-steps, so let's join hands,
not in commiseration but in movement –
I'll make you feel like Fred Astaire, because I know how it is to
stumble through life Romero-esquely!

So we should stay up,
talk about how weird Snoop Dogg is until the early hours,

philosophise as to why and how Dizraeli paints his flowers
and you can sing me your favourite song.

And it's okay if you're drunk and you get all the lyrics wrong.
Just let life be like music, as Langston said.
Apologise for nothing; just let yourself be fed by the food of
love.
Neil Young brings you full to the brim, and Winehouse – that
voice could fix anything.

And I am sorry that I can't hold you quite right,
but I will play you track upon track
until the sky outside turns light
and our eyelashes feel heavy as violin strings,
then we can fall into the peaceful sleep that
only music can bring.

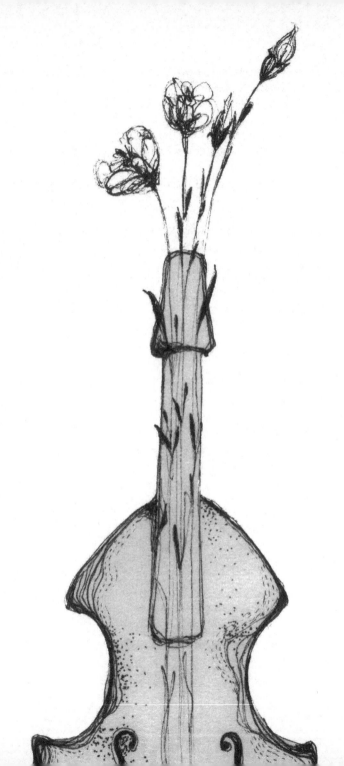

ZENA

for Dana

Your mother was kind to me always,
her scent musky, rich in tones of
violin rosin which gummed the pads
of her thumbs, and I watched with envy
as she would bundle you into an embrace
of which the warmth gleamed off of you both, two
olive and dark figures tightly bound.

You had told me she was a musician, that
was the reason you weren't together always, her
chapped (singing) lips and bruised (moving) feet just could not
stay put.
I would imagine her sitting in dens decked with incense,
cheap, flickering candles, dreadlocks
masking her face – closed-eyed as the music flowed through
the night. Sleeves rolled up, smoke travelling in wreaths
through the air.

You said in the eulogy,
'We made a palace of gold from stone,'
yet in my innocent childhood eyes it was just
beautiful gold.

Veins were veins; tears were tears;
your shared lives now show me something
all the more: stone to gold and trial to love.
Two beautiful women with dark hair
in each other's arms on a futon laced with gold thread.
I will remember you both there.

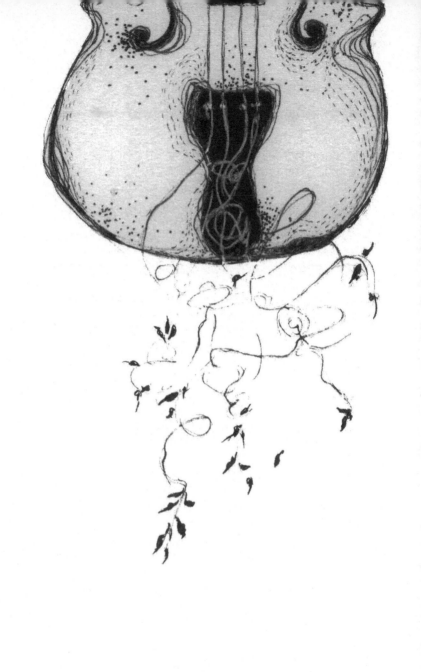

GLUE (PART ONE)

for the street children of Nairobi

His eyes roll back, marbles filled with flame
burning in a head no longer his own,
body limp like overcooked okra
teeters
      falls

            to be stirred into the streets, thick as soup.

The only angel they know is Gabriel,
white face, gilt limbs. That messenger
could never come here, to this petroleum slumber of a town.
So instead they wish for fire-breathing dragons
purring on their bellies, undulating with the warmth of it all.

Children or people? Mouths formed of splinters
wondering if small bodies become big with glue bottles
wedged between blistered lips, chipped pearl tooth,
as though holy. Sniff, soak, spill.

A mother is an absent mirage.

Once you've seen how fumes can strangle the air
you learn not to chase dragons,
but to kiss them.

GLUE (PART TWO)

for the street children of Nairobi

There are worse things in the world, but
it's a good place to start. There are things
heavier than death, though it is where many
people end.

Death's hangover is bitter, like chewing old bark,
splinters on the tongue, inflames the gum,
no one taught us how to swallow.

Bodies cause fires or are fires, my father taught me this.
We watch on.

One eye rolls back.

QUEENIE

after Joseph Moncure March's 'The Wild Party'

Queenie was a blonde,
knew stars from embers
and grazed her
lips on all those bag-eyed angels,
full of tonic & gin,
dressed her chagrin in pearls to dance.

She always awoke with clawing indignity,
a hole where her pride once was,
cold heart strangulation;
in other words, love.
What to do with it?

Dance, thrash in it?
Become the strike, embrace the hit?

Queenie was a blonde
with a lust for fists, their
veins berrylike bulging,
willing to wipe the blood
from her wingtip.

Her man was a clock face,
sweetly round and tightly wound.
They sang together, whiskey-breathed melody,
those old songs, dusty lyrics
lovely tragic.

Together they were balanced vulgarity & wonder.
Together they were the butterflies, boozy eyes and thunder.

ONSLAUGHT

I am not an onslaught.
Defeatism is not an option, and that shit tragedy of your malign life
can lie.

Please allow physical silence before avail;
move swiftly through the grove.
We are taught not to be vain, but are you divine?
These fingertips will touch your creased lips and I will breathe through
the indignity, you can play the lamb whilst I defy the martyr.

There is no shame, just skin. Skin, sweat and the sweetly growing
realisation that we are a gorgeous sin, the thin edge of day will rise
and with no grace, we fade.

I am not an onslaught – five fingers on each hand as I reach to the
sun like a child reaching for its mother's breast, my source of power
came from flesh before it came from light.

Every morning brings with it a brand new me,
eating up the dew left by nightfall, feel the fingers, lingers,
willing change.

These old illuminations rearrange,
taking the form of every body that has ever been against me,
drenched in the sweat of a thousand memories.

I am not an onslaught.
A wicked thing.
Forever troubled and soaked in self-proclaimed pity and sin.

I am not that onset, outpour of tribulations of life, I will never
twist slowly that knife which cut through both your flesh and mine
until we both bled out:
Black and White.

I am not defined by grazes left by vicious playground quarrels,
nor by the lingering sensation of kisses on my inside thigh.

I am not clawing at bed sheets, I am not kissing the moon,

I am not locking eyes with, I am not immune,
I am not coveting riches beyond my control, I am not letting everything go.

I am a martyr, a lamb, a sinner.

I am not an onslaught, I am an eternal beginner.

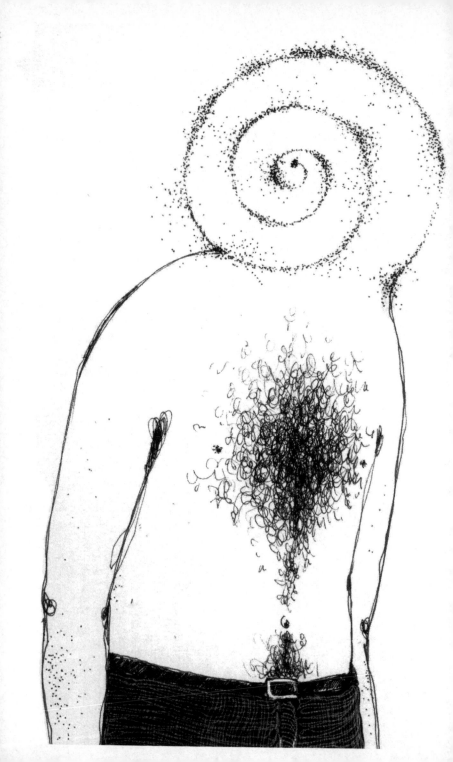

SDRAWKCAB

When your boyfriend tries to kill himself,
not with words and sour looks but with
nooses and needles,
there is nothing poetic about it.

A not-quite-grief creates a film on your skin,
the moist condensation of mist after a long walk.
All of a sudden you're living life backwards
caught in the reverb of those new old songs played over and
over
and over until the words splinter your red wine brain.

The cuffs of your shirt are delicate pink again, sodden through.
Instead of love-tears, all I feel is boredom.

You ate up my heart with refusal to stay;
now my chest waxes like the moon.

OWL & PUSSYCAT

There are air bubbles under your skin
like dried wallpaper. All self-absorbed, self-serving
puncture wounds, gnat-bite redness.
I ask again why you do this.

Is it still to follow in the footsteps of those
sad-eyed musicians you always admired,
whose early graves only added poignancy to the
beauty-scarred lyrics that danced around your head
at fourteen?
Practice rolling joints with shaky hands in your room,
hoping your mum wouldn't walk in to see your chrysalis
shedding
to reveal the mirror image of her ex-lover, same one
whose hands formed into claws and legs bent backwards
in chase of that sticky black tar smack.

I tried to stop writing about you.
But four years is a long time to lose your mind, and now I've
checked
out early. Tried to steady the beat of my heart so that I can
wake
up now before noon, look at the moon with someone
other than you, still feel its beauty.

Too long had we been marooned by the promise of
white rum midnights, honey, money: rolled-up five pound
notes.
And we tried to stop each other from drowning not knowing
the ocean was growing because of our salty tears, my dear,
we were always shipwrecked.
Our own worst enemy.

But don't get me wrong, I still remember nights in front of my
too-small TV. Always full of pizza and beer, my dear,
please don't think I've forgotten.

But a few good nights does not amend cruelty,
as you were to me when I was no help to your recovery.

If I have learnt anything from this little life that we have shared
it's that people aren't there to be saved,
and to try this only causes hurricanes.
Love should not be founded in pain.

Every hope of mine is in you, but I have checked out early.
I'm going to bed early with a cup of green tea
and I smile now, widely.

Love has slipped through my fingers.

Every hope of mine is in you,
this I know you know.
But this is my one last, final sigh
of letting go.

LUCY

There is something decadent
about making cheese toasties
at 5.15 in the morning with lashings of pickle
and a hot chocolate.
The rosé ran out two hours ago.

At this time the sky looks like paper,
crisp writing paper, banned from being used for
drawing, and I feel I could reach up – write a symphony of how
the night fell so quickly.
Hanging out of my bedroom window to smoke joints
we'd gotten other boys to roll,
letting the smoke form ribbons in the midnight air.

Sometimes it felt the sky turned light for us,
other times it felt the sky turned light in spite of us;
we never realised how much time we had.
Lamenting boys with sweaty palms or girls you were not
yet allowed to love.
Talking our sweet tapestry, between episodes of Family Guy,
mouthfuls of salt & vinegar softened by wine.

Suffocating as it could be, there's nothing quite as debonair
as the Devon air.
Where you can see the stars, watch them melt into the white
of day.

It's 5.42.
And with the last crux of the crust,
dabbing of fingers on your plate,

you look at me in that way that says,
Shall we have another one?
My look replies,
*Why not? There are already plenty of crumbs on my bed, and
to be honest I'm not even tired yet.*

THIS IS NOT HOW THE POEMS GO

Kebab meat & chips & mint sauce – £4.80.
Lines traced by cigarette smoke and kisses.
No metaphors, just kisses.
This is not how the poems go,
but it is the start of a new one.

If you were a spirit, I'd mix you only with more
of yourself to last longer and not dilute.
Hands playing each other like keyboards,
searching for something lost or something
new, falling back into that slippery, breathless
quiet.

Watching you sleep is like watching fire burn.
Your body is the one place I cannot touch with words.

So quietly
I melt into you.

DIVISION NONE

I believed life to be a tapestry.
Every thread a person, each stitch a decision,
yet I remember you best with your head balanced
on one calloused hand, the other
measuring out sweet rum that I never liked,
but I liked you. So I downed it in one,
as though you'd poured me your body.

I always knew you would die young.

Not something I should say out loud, but you were so
eager to live that you shot
through life, a bullet made of skin.

And so my love for you (my friend, my friend, my friend) felt
foreign,
like loving a word or a taste that hits the buds of your tongue
in a wisp of air.

SNAILS

I always thought that love would be like Billy Bragg wrote it,
full of tears and joys but ultimately pretty singable.

I've learnt now, and over the years I've found it's impossible
to never let anyone down. And when someone calls you 'love',
it's not always nice. Sometimes it's their well-cultivated device
to make you feel small. I've also learnt that someone's
nastiness
is never all there is to it.

He poured whiskey in my coffee and told me to drink up.
The day was barely sunny, but the way he wore a short-sleeved
shirt
and narrowed his eyes to the clouds made me curious enough
to drink, drink, drink up.

He had scars on his arms like someone I once knew.
I don't know and can't say if it's some sort of pattern,
that I will try to charge in and save the beautiful boys
who despite their sad eyes smile at me.

Well, maybe.
Like when you're a kid and you see a bird with a fractured
wing,
a punctured anatomy.
But by trying to touch it with your tiny hands you impart more
damage, panic and agony.

Perhaps broken boys are like broken birds.
The love you try to force into them only deepens their scars,
which climb up their arms like snail trails on early
morning lawns, those silver streams of slow journeys.

When I was a little girl, I used to pick them up by their shells
to get them to their destination quick.
But then later I'd get sick, a simple thought would click,
anxiety clouded my mind thick.

Maybe, as slow as they had travelled, there was nothing to save.
Perhaps the gift I thought I gave was really an obstacle
to them becoming brave. Brave enough to emancipate them
from their own minds.

But thoughts like these, they are always ill timed.
The minute we decide to stop caring, we care even more.
I think this is one universal and fundamental flaw,
and I know you've heard this so many times before
but you have to try to take those cares
and stick them into something that is only yours.

And don't hate someone because they've hurt you;
by doing that you'll end up hurting someone else, too.
I know that sounds really simple, like a cop-out of a verse,
but it is true. You have to love fairly, kindly.
But, most of all, love you.

I always thought that love would be like Billy Bragg wrote it,
and actually I still think it might be. I also think everyone has
their own individual little key to make something
both beautiful and hideous equally.

Billy was twenty-one years when he wrote that song,
and now somehow I've grown older than that. And I, too,
convince myself I've done everything wrong.
But then I remember it's true what people say:
life only seems really long.

So, fuck it.

Even if you can't sing, sing along.
Do whatever makes you feel like you belong,
and say fuck it!

But at the same time, secretly care all along.
Because caring, caring, living and caring,

that is what makes you strong.

LFM

for Loveday Farmer, Tom Kegode and all the festival kids

In smoke-filled realms we sit,
two dark heads filled with pink wine angled to the floor,
tracing patterns on your carpet, discussing familiar childhoods
spent in fields green and dusty, wherein adults were silly
and children were soldiers.
Set free on the land.

I spent many tiny days with dirty fingernails, hair in dreads
and strung up with beads.
Music hung in the air, a canopy of rhythmic non-symphony that
lay claim to the land in the gentle beats of tumba, of djembe,
mbira, at night; a cacophony of calabash.

Music that spoke of many cultures forming,
did not cry out, 'You are not Maasai, you are not
Ashanti, nor born of sun!'
Merely sang a call to dance, reaching the ears of all
who needed to stretch their limbs through the air and move bodies
in syncopated freedom of expression.

Sometimes my brother and I grew weary of the self-proclaimed
selfless yet self-indulgent lifestyles of white men
with blonde dreadlocks.
We longed for bottles of Sprite, plastic bread and too long
in front of the television.
Being surrounded so entirely by beautiful nature and never-ending
music can be suffocating.

But as you said, as you cracked your knuckles expertly,
we were soldiers.
Children meeting children in an open field, no questions asked
about the formalities of friendship.

Just a call to arms, bare feet stomping through patchy grass
chasing butterflies, making swords from sticks,
wasting away the lazy days.
I would not write these days of childhood in any other way.

HOME
For Josh Levontine

You rarely reply to my text messages.
I'm used to this.
You're like a bird who although it has a house built –
full of soft cotton wool and feed – cannot stop stretching its
wings.
So I swiftly deny the neuroses that have tendencies to envelop
my character to remember you're just off flying somewhere,
and for a fleeting moment in the coming days or months
the breeze may prove too chilly and you might come down to
rest.

I like to rest.
More old cat than young sparrow, my energy goes mostly into
perfecting cups of tea.
For me: Assam. Milk. No sugar. In a mug made of firm ridged
china.
More likely to be reading a book in the summer than
playing Frisbee, sometimes I wonder why you still
appear to like me, 'cause I'm no globetrotter like you.

Though I wish I was, because I do believe that change is key
to happiness and being free, but I find meeting new people
scary. I'm shy and awkward company; I crave kindness
and conversation, but it's tricky when your tongue is trapped
by terrified train of thoughts of inadequacy.

I think, though, you know this. And that every smile you throw
willing strangers and beat you drop a foot down to is your way
of
quelling the quiet quandaries of not good enough that beat
their rhythm in your head.

We all need a break from it.
Carousels of doubt that are anxiety-fed.
We both have our medicine,
yours is people and mine paper.
I think we're both guilty of staying up
later than we should just to worry.

And I'd prefer for you to be happy.

So I can forgive the untapped texts, and weeks of
silence, as long as when you come home
you're smiling and have some stories to tell me.
I don't have much to offer but I can make you a
bloody good cup of tea.
For you I think masala chai, two sugars maybe.

This is how I know you are a friend indeed,
that we're not about need but willing,
and that months can form between us but in no time we can
fill it in
with wine, music, laughter and remembering
how sweet it is to be at home
in your own skin.

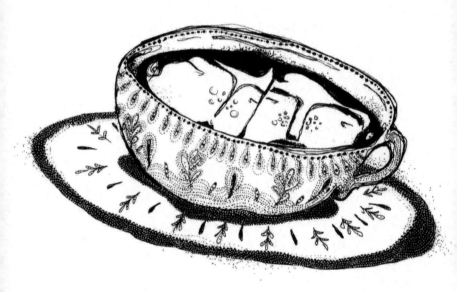

CHERRY

for Handina Dutiro

It starts off slow before it picks up speed.
It starts with baby clothes, progresses to scraped knees,
then before you know it you're at top speed trying to be the
person
you want to be and you deserve it.
To look in the mirror and like it, but it is painful,
this journey is not all soft focus and bright lights,
sometimes doubt comes in.

So listen:
not everything is beautiful,
bad things can happen that can't be made good, that's okay.
Hold on to let go, hold on to let go, hold on to let go.

You can be scared sometimes. Just remember to breathe;
it's a skill that can't be taught, it's not tangible but you can feel
it.
Skin is a healer, and the sky is massive!

And you are small, so small but never insignificant.
You have loved so much, it has made loving an element.
You are special, your soul is the best I've seen
and when it smiles shows dimples

But when you are tired come in, trust the world can be gentle.
You could go on for miles, but for now come in.
So I can hold you.

Once you learn being alone is not lonely, you are never alone
unless you want to be.
Think of leaves falling from trees, think of fire, like velvet.

Think of things that are not metaphors,
beauty in its own right.

These words will not move mountains,
they may rarely see the light of day.

I just hope they make it easier
for you to just be today.

Because I know accumulating steps
and breaths feels like day-to-day torment.
Strive to remember and strive to believe that you are
more than heaven-sent.

Whatever shades the grass may be, it will always be green,
and I cannot help but love the sun, who shines down bright
and warm despite all it has seen.

GOODNITE

Everything looks better in the moonlight,
brighter too.

Peaceful somehow, and I wonder it's true what they say,
that you can pray the rain away.
Because if I'm going to dance in it, I think I'd like to do it with you.

Take off our socks and shoes, feel the earth between our toes and
let loose our limbs until the downpour slows in rhythm of
our movement.

I think this is what life should be about,
and all the nervous twitches and worry are just filler
for something conceived of waste.
Life should taste sweeter than tears after all,
so when we're feeling insignificant and small,
we should make as much noise as possible,
even if your voice is quiet.

We should say thank you more often.

Did anyone ever tell you that you're made of star dust?
That's not just poetry, that's a kind of science.
I think that's pretty cool,
and makes life that little bit more worth sparkling in.

REQUITE

We are unexpected
and sweet.
Nectarines and hash,
dark hair,
soft, smiling.

Breathing in the resin of your body,
blue-eyed, long-limbed, smoky monkey boy.
No one could ever plan these tumbling moments.

You read me stories of your past in nature, I make them
poems:
'What a fool you've made of me,
grown around and taken me down,
my golden fig tree.'

I only came around for pasta bake after the pub.

I loved your shoulders most of all,
they were like maps.

If this were a film we'd sing something fitting and beautiful;
instead we sing 'No Diggity' and get told off by your flatmate.

This is the last time I saw you.
You are safe here.
I'll keep you here.

TWO GIRLS IN LOVE ON A BUS

It's not because the sky is blue that it is beautiful,
just as it's not the green of your eyes that makes you irresistible,
but the timbre of your voice and the smoothness of skin that dips
between your clavicle.

And how with imperfect hands the desire to touch is like trying to
stroke clouds or paint the stars.

They say all this without speaking,
and get off at Sefton Park Road.

DAUGHTER SKY

a story and a song

Packed my bags again last night,
a pattern that's become so easy,
forming lyrics in my brain that say it's time to go home.

Everything looks brighter in the moonlight somehow,
and it's blue-grey clouds up above say in their delicate,
raindrop-laced way it's time to go home,
to go home again.

My mother was the sun and my father the moon,
and I, the daughter of the sky.
Dragonfly eyes,
voice soft as a sigh

A life like this becomes painfully daunting,
so one day I grew legs and I started walking.

And my father said to me,
Where will you go?
When the seasons pass too slow, child,
it's harder to fall into the sky
than out of it.

***

She never really had a name,
her father called her sun-drop
or her mother star-shine.

To others she was simply Daughter Sky.
Growing up amongst the clouds sounds
like a dream.
But as we know, once you're a teen
and the world throbs with terrifying, beguiling, beautiful
promise, the place you have always been becomes prison.
Besides, the sky is always wet.

When your mother is the sun, your father the moon,
you are some transparent thing, dark yet light,
cold but warm.
Daughter Sky wanted something of her own, and the endless
green and blue below looked gift-wrapped for her.

So she waited until next rainfall and tumbled

between the endless drops.

The earth was like her, that cold which
burrowed into depths of warmth.
Intoxicating.
Daughter Sky's entire body spread across the land, darkening
in tall, echolike movements between the trees and rocks and
buildings.

She felt like music, she had become everything.
For everything is always changing, moving, and melting into
shadow.

From the sky it is hard to see land.
Sun and moon circle the earth
in hopes of finding their daughter
who enriches the dark of her father,
stretches in the warmth of her mother

but never hears them sing:

Where will you go?
When the seasons pass too slow, child,
it's harder to fall into the sky
than out of it.

CAB CALLOWAY

I fell in love with a black and white image,
washing-machine limbs.
Hi-de-hi-de-hi-de-ho!

His smile reminds me of the space where furniture once was.
Busy emptiness, his is the face of a child missing.

Eternally ageless – held up by silver platitudes and dancing feet.

I imagine Cab a young man,
the whiskey-in-water-bottles kind of kid,
turtle walking the room,
a Romeo who lived.

And that song he sings.

Poor Min, eternally stuck inside a grin and swagger.
Poor Min, tongue rhythmic tales of grandeur – I see her,

the kind of girl with foundation too light.
The type of woman that boys
write about saving one day, but they never stay.

So she becomes a story, a poem, a call and response
at 2am closing time.

Her boys romanticise sadness and bathtub gin,
while Poor Min is out in the cold again, trying to get in.

Cab Calloway lifts the microphone to his lips,
it's tender and intimate,
almost a kiss.

14/11/15

Mulled cider supped, film digested,
analysed. A cigarette break carries more
death than usual.
We hear:
a terrorist attack on Paris.
We flick ash and sigh: Aaahh.

Go back to mulled cider, Friday night but
work in the morning.

Stumble home with wet toes to sleep, all the
clouds are wrung out grey, the thud thud thud
of bass loiters in the air

When the sky is morning-pale, skinned of night,
a girl in coal hijab sits on my bus.
Her eyes are like bullet holes. I want to reach
out to her, say, I know, I know, I know it's not your fault.

I don't,
of course.
I press the bell at my stop.

Photos are overlaid red, blue, white.
Facebook shares a photo of a boy, his head red ribbons,
his father's knees damp with ash-fuelled tears.
I cannot stomach this relishing of terror,
the one-upmanship of tragedy.

I think of you,
Paris, Beirut, Syria, Iraq, Japan.
I try to picture your fingerprints.

We walk a tightrope of shame.
In life, no one taught us how to handle death.

Think of the lives of the deaths.
Think of the girl, first time allowed into that club.
Wonder what it felt like to make her smile.

Think of the man who left the match early to kiss his daughter
goodnight.
Think of the couple, just wanted chips, then to go home
and watch TV, three weeks together, when holding hands still felt
like quivering
vibrations.

Think of the lives of the deaths,
their beautiful, human
idiosyncrasies.

Think of their lives
and throw hands in the air,
not in surrender but in dance, in prayer.

Singing, to all gods and mortals who will hear,
We live for peace, we live for peace.

Hope that it travels.
Hope that we are louder than bombs.

ORIGAMI

These pavements are pages of a story I know well,
framed the faces of all the boys and girls I once loved.
I was soft-lipped, tobacco-stained and without purpose;
at sixteen what could be sweeter than that?

When I come back and breathe in the salted air, I can still
taste the memories: Conversed feet dangling the harbour's precipice,
our lives then were all music, Monster Munch and milky vodka.

Paris got a flat on Embankment Road where we would
drink thick, fortified wine and listen to every Bob Dylan cassette his
dad left behind
when he took that final trip, tiptoed into oblivion.
Paris never cried about it.
He made movies from his memories and taught me how to roll
cigarettes.

He took care of me.
I think because I never asked if he was okay,
but sat close next to him when he wasn't,
to keep the demons at bay.

We were thick as thieves, trickling down North Hill with fake IDs,
whiskey in water bottles and menthol tips.

One of these rouged-up nights I lost my virginity to a gin-eyed boy
who smelled like mephedrone and must.
I never loved him, though; I just loved the things that made him up:
William Blake tattoo emblazoned on his chest, calloused hands and
crumpled-up hoodies.

The arty boy, a rollie eternally lounging out of his lips, the body of a
man before his brain had caught up.

I can still remember how the smell of him would make me gorgeously
giddy, like drinking beer in bed.

Sometimes I wonder what might have happened if we had fallen in
love.

Skittered across Plymouth's cobbled streets holding hands and pressing cold cheek to cold cheek.

Maybe I'd have stayed: turned a blind eye to his roving one and we'd watch the waves until our hair turned grey and we got sick of each other, but even sicker without one another.
That static life never sat right with me, so I left it all behind.

The shrinking streets of my memories returned to crashing waves –
Plymouth was no longer mine.
Nothing but bombed-out, rebuilt, happy shopper crowd fodder with an angry sea attached, for good measure.

Cider puddled in the gaps between the cobbles, sailors on leave seeking their sirens in Vodka Revs and twenty-four-hour breakfasts.
Paris moved to London's sharp edges, high-rises, Saturday nights drinking £12 cocktails.
I think he is happy there, blue eyes in the bustle.
I moved to Bristol – full of love and music and dancing,
finally not feeling sore anymore.

But I folded Plymouth into origami,
memorised the kisses and scrapes,
the crushed-up lines and nights in with mates
like a script.

Each fold is a face, each bend is a memory of a time and a place.
So if I fear my past has faded,
if I somehow forgot it,
I folded Plymouth into origami,
and keep it safely in my pocket.

SWEETS - FOR THE SWEET

I was so used to thinking backwards,
to drinking fire, skipping breakfast.

I was so used to being scared and
dwelling on the past.

I was so used to sickness, and being
three grams deep.

I was so used to acid reflux and distorted sleep.

But you came along and said,

Sweets, for the sweet,
to love yourself is no mean feat.

But if I can do it, so can you,
just watch carefully – do what I do.

And your face was a creased lead scribble,
I could almost trace the lines.
You took the cruelty from your life,
and turned it into kind.

Life has been hard sometimes,
but I still find myself here.
I'm trying to write the truth,
to overcome the fear.

I'm relearning myself, with every new heartbeat,
I'm getting used to feeling like a person,
feeling more concrete.

Hoping one day I can be the one to say,
to whoever might need it,

Sweets, for the sweet,
to love yourself is no mean feat.

But if I can do it, so can you,
just watch carefully – do what I do.

12 WEST STREET

for Mama

Home is not the precipice you make it into,
not quite so tangible that you could
fall in or out without knowing.

Home is the fur between the floorboards,
the books stuffed sloppily on shelves,
clattering claws on wooden staircases,
smells of toast, rose moisturiser
and incense.
It is that quiver in the throat, impossible to
swallow, and music in the kitchen.

Stories of home got lost on the way back.
And somehow, forgotten are the shadows, etched into memory.
But still there is that whisper of breadth
of change in small spaces.
I like my stories stretched over time,
tangled in dirty towels.
In places no one else can reach.

These secret stories of home,
spoken soft, swift, sweet.
Between the laundered sheets.

ACKNOWLEDGEMENTS

Thank you to Burning Eye Books for the belief and support.

Thank you to my original poetry fam, Saskia Tomlinson and Graham Chilcott, and to my extended fam, the poets of Bristol. In particular thank you to Tom Denbigh, Sam Grudgings and Beth Calverley for your editing help.

Thank you to Roundhouse and the inimitably wonderful Liz Counsell for Words First. My most potent, pungent, chewy love and thanks to the Raleigh Road Collective for reminding me of my love for poetry.

Thanks to Apples and Snakes, Arvon Lumb Bank and Tobacco Factory Theatres.

Thank you to Lucy Rhodes, for your patience and friendship, and Loveday Farmer for the pink wine and encouragement.

Thank you to Ed Strong – you're my fave.

And of course, thank you to my entire mad family; to Dad and to Raybo. Most of all thank you to the Cobwebs crew: Mama, Dina, Tom, Steve and Gertie, for filling me full of love that spills out into poetry.